CONTENT

Special Offer Awaits!

Ready for something special? **Scan the QR** code and **JOIN OUR COMMUNITY** to receive your **FREE GIFT**. It's our way of saying **THANK YOU** for connecting with us. Act now and enjoy this exclusive offer!

CHAPTER I: EARLY LIFE ADVENTURES

Birth and Family

Once upon a time, on July 6, 1907, in a place called Coyoacán in Mexico, a girl was born with a flowery name, Frida Kahlo. Her father, Guillermo, was a German photographer and her mother, Matilde, had Spanish and Native Mexican heritage. Frida Kahlo and her three sisters grew up in La Casa Azul, a house full of Mexican culture and art.

Although her early life was filled with health problems, it was also marked by love and adventure. She wandered the garden of La Casa Azul, using her imagination and love of nature, which would later fill her artwork with deep cultural meaning.

Childhood Adventures

From a young age, Frida had a strong sense of adventure. She cherished exploring La Casa Azul's verdant gardens, where she was inspired by the beauty of the natural world, flowers and animals. Without a doubt, this inspiration influenced her career throughout.

She had polio when she was six years old, but her enthusiasm never wavered. She took pride in how she embraced her physical limits and always found a way to interact with her surroundings. The support of her family eased her journey and, in a unique way, contributed to her forging a close bond with the natural world.

3

Growing Up in Coyoacán

Frida grew up surrounded by Mexican folklore, music and dance, because there were local festivals and events in Coyoacán. For example, in the main square, there were groups of cowboys who sang and danced while playing mariachi music. All of these experiences contributed to Frida's artistic life.

The cultural life of the neighborhood of Coyoacán, where Frida lived, was an important part of her self-definition as she embraced her roots. She learned to love the color, sound and narrative of her life, which was later reflected in her art. Thanks to this vibrant cultural life, she felt a deep sense of belonging and pride in her Mexican identity.

6

Influences of Mexican Culture

From childhood, Frida was immersed in and identified with Mexican culture. She participated in traditional festivals, folk art and indigenous customs, all of which influenced her intuitive sense of design and artistic imagination.

In addition, Mexican culture shaped the themes of Frida's work. Her art often explored traditional Mexican folklore, mythology and daily life, celebrating her Mexican identity. Frida's work exemplified her belief that "in the future, someone will have to write that the past of the world belongs to Mexico," linking Mexican identity to the world.

CHAPTER 2: OVERCOMING CHALLENGES

Health Struggles

Frida Kahlo's physical and psychological troubles began early. At the age of six, she contracted polio, which caused her to develop a limp and made her feel like an outsider. Despite this, Frida was a determined young girl. She engaged in physical activities to strengthen her leg and her father encouraged her to play sports such as soccer and swimming, unheard of for girls at the time.

These activities fortified her for the challenges to come. Her childhood illness also played a key role in shaping her character and art. Frida's determination to overcome her debilitating illness was an early example of the tenacity to walk again after the accident.

A Bad Accident Happened

By 18, Frida had a terrible bus accident that broke her spine, collarbone, ribs, pelvis and fractured her right leg and foot. From then on, Frida transformed her pain and suffering into her art. Her physical pain was intense and had to go through many surgeries and long periods of recovery.

Despite all the pain, Frida's spirit stayed strong. Painting helped her express her pain and show her resilience. Through her art, she discovered that creativity could be a powerful way to overcome tough times. This accident marked her adolescence and her life in general.

Recovery and Resilience

Frida's long and difficult recovery involved many surgeries and months of being in bed, but painting helped her through it all. She painted self-portraits that showed not only her pain but also her strength and resilience.

What made Frida's resilience so special was that she not only survived her continuous challenges, but continued to paint and even thrived. Her paintings became a way for her to express her emotions, pain and bravery. Even when things were very tough, Frida found the strength to be creative. She was, and still is, a true inspiration.

Discovering Inner Strength

Frida always found her inner strength and courage. Her illness and the accident were very tough on her, but she always found a way to keep going. She learned to love herself and express her inner world and strength through her art.

Frida's journey was one of self-discovery and empowerment. She learned to channel her pain into her art and, through the power of self-expression, turned her suffering into artwork of profound inspiration. Her legacy proves that even in the darkest of times, the human spirit can rise up, discovering unique beauty and lasting meaning.

CHAPTER 3: DISCOVERING ART

Her First Paintings

After recovering from the bus accident, Frida began painting. She started with simple subjects, like portraits and still lifes, capturing the scenes around her on canvas. Bedridden for months and in pain, she discovered her talent for painting when she created her first still life while lying in bed at 22 years old.

As Frida continued to paint whenever she felt well, she gained confidence and her technique improved, as did her subjects. Her early paintings were not remarkable, but they served as the foundation for her later masterpieces. Each brushstroke helped her express feelings she couldn't put into words.

Art as Therapy

Painting became her therapy; the pain and trauma she endured after her accident seemed to disappear when she was painting. Her canvases became an expression of her inner emotions: bright colors and strong, chaotic feelings.

Little by little, symbols from her life appeared in her paintings. Her artwork can be seen as a form of art therapy, helping her cope with the emotional and physical effects of her challenges. Through her art, Frida was able to express her feelings and share them with others.

Develloping Her Style

Gradually, as Frida's confidence grew, she began to experiment more with her techniques and subjects. Inspired by Mexican culture and folk art, she integrated reality and imagination into her work to create her own identity and develop a unique style.

Her style became more self-referential and intimate, filled with surreal elements that reflected her physical and emotional pain. This body of work played a crucial role in her self-fashioning as an artist, allowing her to express her innermost feelings and experiences in a way that resonated deeply with viewers.

20

Early Inspirations

From the start, Frida Kahlo's inspiration came from her Mexican roots and her own life. She was fascinated by the bright colors and symbolic motifs of Mexican folk art, which infused her own favorite compositions. The Mexican landscape and its artistic traditions also inspired her.

Her exposure to other artists' works, especially those of her peers who embraced Mexican culture, fueled her creativity. Some of Frida's early paintings showed the influence of these works, blending traditional styles with her own imaginative interpretations, a mixture that set her on the path to her unique style.

21

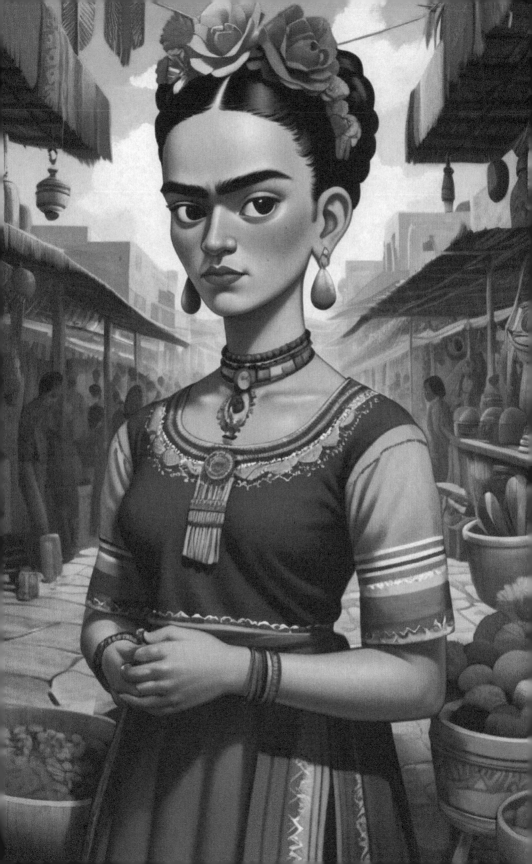

CHAPTER 4: LOVE AND MARRIAGE

Meeting Diego Rivera

Frida Kahlo first met Diego Rivera when she was a young art student. Diego was already a famous painter known for his large murals. Frida admired his work and often asked for his advice about her own paintings. They quickly became friends and eventually fell in love due to their shared passion for painting. Diego recognized her as a kindred spirit and encouraged her to keep painting.

Their first meeting marked the start of a complex and passionate relationship. Diego became not only her teacher but also her partner in life and art. Their connection was deep and immediate, leading to a lifelong collaboration that influenced both of their art careers.

Marriage and Collaborations

Frida and Diego were married in 1929 despite objections from friends and family. Their relationship was an artistic partnership of equals, with each encouraging and inspiring the other. They worked together, borrowing ideas and techniques from one another.

Despite occasional strain in their marriage, their passion for art kept them together. They frequently painted side by side, learning from and inspiring each other. Their marriage was a blend of passion, creativity and respect as both artists benefited from the other's presence.

Traveling Together

They also traveled extensively, especially to the US and Europe. These trips gave them opportunities to exhibit their work and meet artists abroad. Frida and Diego were inspired by new cultures and ideas, which they incorporated into their art.

As much as she enjoyed traveling, Frida missed her home and country. She painted to capture her mood and the new things she saw. Traveling together helped their relationship and enriched their work. Their time abroad influenced their art in many ways, introducing new themes and techniques that made their paintings even more unique.

Artistic Influence

The large-scale public murals of Diego and the personal, intimate paintings of Frida nourished each other's work. Frida's paintings became more expressive and bold, while Diego's murals grew more personal and emotional. They pushed each other to experiment and develop their art, making their work more memorable and impactful.

Their artistic legacy lives on through the many artists inspired by their work. Frida and Diego showed the power of a creative partnership and worked as a team to change the course of art history. They demonstrated how two artists could influence each other.

CHAPTER 5: PERSONAL LIFE AND STRUGGLES

Challenges in Marriage

Frida Kahlo and Diego Rivera's marriage had some ups and downs. They adored each other, but they had a rocky relationship. Diego was unfaithful and this often tested Frida's patience. However, they inspired one another, supported each other through their art and shared countless creative moments.

Although their journey was not easy, they continued to support each other through art projects and exhibitions. Their complex relationship was a big part of their lives and showed their dedication and devotion to their art. They remained important to each other, even during the tough times.

Personal Pain from Frida

Besides physical pain, Frida Kahlo was also emotionally affected by her personal issues. Her paintings reflect her marriage problems and ongoing health issues. The way Frida felt about her problems was expressed on canvas, helping her cope with her hardships.

Her paintings were often an expression of her feelings and a way of recording her personal conflicts. By externalizing her pain through art, she was able to communicate her experiences and understand her emotions. Her work became a channel for her feelings and an expression of her pain.

Grief and Loss from Frida

Throughout her life, Frida suffered many losses. She felt sad when people she knew died and this influenced her art and how she viewed the world. Even though she was sad, she expressed her sadness through her art in a way that celebrated the people she lost.

Frida's paintings were often an expression of her grief and an attempt to find meaning in her life. She was strong in creating beautiful art while feeling sad and through her work she found ways to express herself and cope with her losses.

Friendships and Support

Despite a difficult life, Frida was uplifted by her friends and pets. She had many friends who encouraged her to keep creating and a small group of dogs who loved and cuddled with her, providing comfort and joy when she was feeling down. Friends visited her at La Casa Azul to talk, laugh, share ideas and enjoy the company of her dogs, who stayed close and offered affection.

These visits and her pets' companionship were vital for Frida. They brought her happiness and inspiration, helping her stay positive and motivated. Through their support, Frida found strength and comfort, which played a crucial role in her life.

35

CHAPTER 6: ACTIVISM AND SOCIAL ENGAGEMENT

Political Involvement

Frida Kahlo believed in fairness and equality. This is why she joined the Mexican Communist Party, which aimed that everyone had the same opportunities and was treated in the same way. Frida thought that with the help of other people, society could become a better place.

Her political convictions not only shaped the actions she took, but also the way she painted. Frida's art was used to highlight social problems and expressed her support for the causes in which she believed. It was by engaging in politics that Frida tried to move others to consider issues of fairness and inequality.

Support for Social Causes

Frida cared about workers and indigenous people. She supported them and fought for their rights. She attended rallies and joined protests to raise her voice against injustice. Frida was always willing to take a stand.

Frida's social activism inspired many others. Her dedication to standing up for the rights of those who are often overlooked set an example of unity and mutual support. Frida believed that rights should be fought for, not just given. Her actions showed the importance of working together to achieve fairness and equality.

Friendship with León Trotsky

Frida and Diego Rivera hosted the exiled leader Léon Trotsky in their home in Mexico. They discussed politics and world events at length, developing mutual respect for each other's ideas. Trotsky's experiences abroad greatly influenced Frida's beliefs.

The friendship with Trotsky also influenced Frida's art. She drew on the concepts and themes from their discussions and this mix of personal experience and new ideas made her work exciting during this time. Frida's artwork began to reflect her deepening understanding of global issues, combining personal and political themes in a unique and powerful way.

Art as a Voice for Change

Frida's art carried a social and political message. If she felt strongly about a particular issue, her work expressed it through powerful symbols of the struggle for justice and equality. Frida's work is not just beautiful; it is beautiful because of its message about the world.

Her paintings were a call to action, urging others to think about and address social issues. In this way, she demonstrated how art can be a powerful force for change. Frida's ability to combine beauty with a strong message made her artwork both impactful and inspiring.

CHAPTER 7: IDENTITY AND CULTURE

Themes in Her Work

Themes of pain, love and identity are important in many of Frida Kahlo's paintings. She painted about her life, feelings and experiences, making her work very personal. This personal nature is its strength, attracting people with the emotions she expresses. Her distinctive style also stands out.

Frida's art allowed her to express and explore complex feelings and ideas. Through her art, we see the physical and emotional struggles she faced, as well as her resilience and strength. Her art tells her story and reveals her inner world, making her experiences and emotions visible to all.

45

Cultural Influences

Frida was passionate about her Mexican heritage; she loved the traditional clothing, jewelry and art of Mexico. Her work celebrated these beautiful aspects of Mexican culture.

By drawing inspiration from her heritage and borrowing symbols from fellow artists, Frida made her art unique by incorporating her own voice. Her paintings are deeply personal and feel like an homage to Mexico, blending tradition and innovation. This combination of personal expression and cultural celebration is what makes her work so distinctive and powerful, highlighting her love for her country and its artistic traditions.

Frida's Self-Portraits

It is said that most of Frida's work consisted of self-portraits. This was an intimate way for her to create her identity and express her inner feelings. She used her own appearance and life events to depict a story about herself and her emotions.

Frida's self-portraits narrate the story of her life, including her triumphs and traumas, her beauty and flaws, her strength and fragility, as well as her anger and humor. Her art has made Frida Kahlo's life visible to us. Her self-portraits invite us to confront her closely, revealing so much of her essence that, when we look at them, we feel as though we truly know her.

Symbolism and Meaning

Frida's paintings are rich with symbolism. Symbols were the core expressive principle of her art, allowing her to narrate her life through paint. By using symbolism, she could fill her paintings with deeper meaning and add layers of significance to even the smallest details. Her symbols were direct expressions of her thoughts and emotions.

Understanding the visual symbols in Kahlo's work reveals that what might initially seem like a simple or beautiful image is actually rich with meaning and insight. Her paintings are not just visually striking; they challenge viewers to look deeper.

49

CHAPTER 8: GROWING RECOGNITION

New York and Paris

Her work was exhibited in New York and Paris. In 1938, she had a notable exhibition at the Julien Levy Gallery in New York, where she received widespread praise from critics and art lovers. This exposure helped her reach a broader audience and gain recognition outside Mexico.

In 1939, she showcased her work in Paris, where she met influential artists like Pablo Picasso and Marcel Duchamp. Her unique style and themes surprised and impressed many. These international exhibitions were crucial for establishing Frida's presence in the global art scene.

First Solo Exhibition

Her first solo exhibition opened at the Galería de Arte Mexicano in Mexico City in 1953. Frida was overjoyed to have her work displayed to such a wide audience. Despite her own health struggles, she attended the opening in an ambulance.

The exhibition was a tremendous success and Frida became the talk of the town. Many people came to see her intense, often provocative and emotionally charged paintings. This event marked the beginning of several moments when she was celebrated as a groundbreaking artist. Frida's bold, unapologetic self-expression established her as a star.

International Acclaim

As Frida Kahlo's paintings were exhibited worldwide, she gained widespread acclaim. Art scholars and critics began to appreciate her unique style, marked by vivid colors and intense emotions. Her work resonated with audiences globally, bringing her international fame.

Her growing renown led to her paintings being acquired by major galleries and museums around the world. Frida's Mexican identity and personal history were celebrated as key elements of her art. This recognition underscored how deeply her cultural and personal experiences influenced her creations, securing her place in art history.

Impact on the Art World

Her style and themes have left a lasting impact on the art world and continue to inspire contemporary artists. Frida Kahlo's work stands out for its blend of personal pain with cultural and political themes, giving her art a distinct signature and a deep connection with viewers.

Beyond her technique, Frida's courage and determination have inspired many to use art to share their own stories. Her legacy lives on in the way she broke boundaries and opened new paths for artists, particularly women and those from marginalized communities.

CHAPTER 9: LATER LIFE YEARS

Continued Health Battles

As Frida grew older, she began to suffer from a variety of health problems. She underwent surgery and treatments frequently and was often in pain. But these issues did not stop her. Frida continued to paint despite the illnesses she suffered, from her childhood to her adult life.

She was a survivor. Frida wouldn't let her physical setbacks define her. Instead, she turned her pain into art, visually portraying her experiences and feelings. She continued to create and she was able to inspire other people. This is a real proof about her dedication and love for painting.

Art During Adversity

Despite all the suffering Frida endured, she continued to paint and some of her best work emerged in her later years. The Broken Column (1944) and Without Hope (1946) express not only her pain and joy but also her remarkable artistry. These works are often considered her most personal and significant, capturing her suffering while conveying powerful messages of endurance and triumph.

Frida's ability to transform pain into beauty captivated audiences worldwide, showcasing her extraordinary resilience and creativity. Her art not only documents her experiences but also inspires others to face their own challenges with courage.

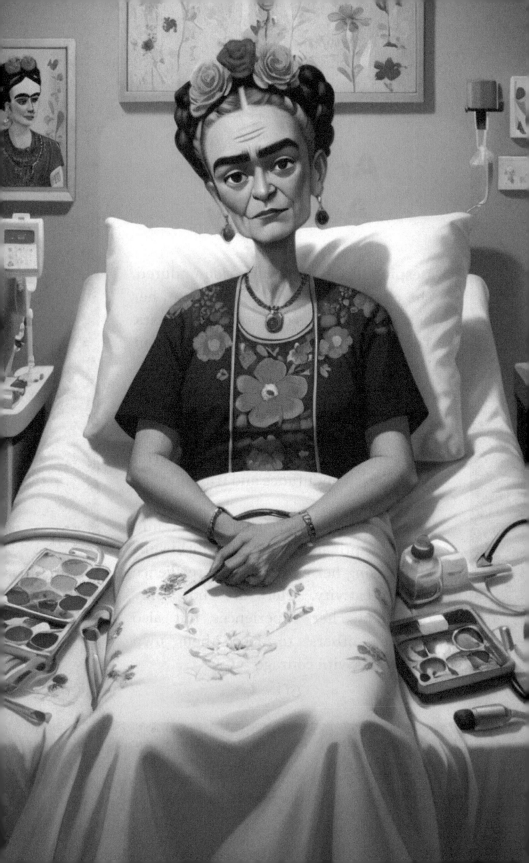

Her Final Works

As Frida's health declined, her art remained a powerful source of strength and expression. She created some of her final works as a testament to her enduring spirit, including the painting Viva la Vida just before her death.

These last paintings are admired for their vibrant energy and emotional depth. Despite her suffering, Frida continued to paint with passion. Her final artworks are a testament to her resilience and artistry, showing how she transformed her pain into beauty. Frida's ability to create such moving pieces, even in her last days, highlights her remarkable strength and dedication to her craft.

Lasting Legacy
Frida

Unfortunately, Frida Kahlo did not live too long. She passed away in 1954, aged 47, but her star shines brightly. She is still an inspiration for artists, feminists and those who feel like outsiders. Her art, her image and her person remains alive 70 years after her death and she will still be an icon and an example for many years.

Today, her former home, La Casa Azul, is a museum dedicated to her life and work and a permanent reminder of her spirit. Her story and her art remind us of the amazing resilience of the human spirit and to never give up, regardless of the circumstances.

CHAPTER 10:
FRIDA'S ENDURING IMPACT

Influence on Modern Art

Frida's art and painting technique, characterized by a bold use of color and an effective depiction of emotions, continues to be impactful today. Many contemporary works show the influence of Frida Kahlo's personal style, as well as her ability to express universal personal and cultural themes.

Moreover, Frida's self-portraits are iconic. Viewers, particularly modern artists looking to challenge traditional notions of beauty and identity, are inspired by her work and encouraged to experiment with painting and other forms of digital media to express and define their own identities and experiences.

65

Frida: A Feminist Icon

Frida Kahlo is recognized as a feminist heroine. Her life and art overturned many conventions, especially those pertaining to gender and identity. Her unflinching self-expression and her recovery from the serious challenges of her life have deep resonance within feminist movements both here and abroad.

Her paintings frequently touch on themes of female empowerment and autonomy. By exposing her own suffering and vulnerabilities, Frida has helped many women find their voice. She continues to be an inspiration for women of all generations as a liberated and emancipated icon.

Celebration of Her Life

The life of Frida Kahlo is celebrated through exhibitions, books, films, documentaries and, of course, every year on her birthday with commemorative events and activities. Her life story remains a source of inspiration around the world and her artistic and cultural legacy endures.

Such celebrations focus on her art and her fortitude. Festivals and exhibitions devoted to Frida Kahlo showcase her art and tell her story to new generations. Her memory must be cultivated and kept alive, lest it be forgotten.

Global Cultural Icon

Her image and work are now synonymous with Mexican culture as well as creative expression worldwide. Her distinctive style, replete with bold colors and Mexican imagery, is celebrated across the globe, while her face (sometimes embellished with flowers) is ubiquitous in popular culture.

From murals and street art to clothing and merchandise, Frida's likeness is appropriated by countless producers. She serves as an intertextual reference point for fashion, music, popular feminism and activism. Frida's legacy as a global cultural icon continues to expand.

First paper book edition June 2024

Published by:

Great Minds Press